THE MARKETING MAVERICK

Revamping Your Start-Up's Advertising Strategies

Korki Levine

CONTENTS

DISCLAIMER

The information contained within this book is intended for informational purposes only and should not be construed as legal or professional advice. The authors and publishers of this book are not responsible for any losses or damages that may arise from the use of the information contained within.

The reader assumes full responsibility for any decisions made based on the information in this book. The authors and publishers do not endorse any particular service or product mentioned in this book and are not responsible for any consequences resulting from their use.

The reader should exercise caution and discretion when implementing the advice and strategies outlined in this book, and should be aware of the potential risks and consequences. This book is not a substitute for professional or legal advice and should not be relied upon as such.

By reading and using the information in this book, the reader acknowledges and agrees to hold harmless the authors, publishers, and any other parties involved in the creation or distribution of this book from any and all liability, claims, damages, or losses that may arise from their use of the information contained herein.

CHAPTER 1: UNDERSTANDING THE BASICS OF MARKETING

Hey there! Welcome to the first chapter of "The Marketing Maverick - Revamping Your Start-Up's Advertising Strategies." In this chapter, we're going to dive into the exciting world of marketing and explore its importance for start-ups. So, grab a cup of coffee (or your beverage of choice) and let's get started!

Defining Marketing and Its Importance for Start-Ups

Now, you might be thinking, "What exactly is marketing?" Well, my friend, marketing is much more than just advertising. It encompasses all the activities and strategies that a business undertakes to promote its products or services and attract customers. From market research to branding, from advertising to customer relationship management, marketing touches every aspect of your start-up's growth.For start-ups, marketing is particularly crucial. When you're just starting out, you need to create awareness about your business and build a customer base. You could have the most amazing product or service, but if no one knows about it, your business is going to struggle. That's where marketing comes in -- it helps you reach your target audience, communicate your value proposition, and ultimately drive sales.

Identifying the Target Audience and Their Needs

Now that we understand the importance of marketing for start-ups, let's focus on one of the fundamental aspects of marketing: the target audience. Who are your ideal customers? What do they need or want? What problems can your product or service solve for them?

Understanding your target audience is like holding a compass that guides all your marketing efforts. By creating detailed buyer personas and conducting market research, you can gain valuable insights into your customers' preferences, behaviours, and pain points. This knowledge will help you tailor your marketing messages, choose the right advertising channels, and deliver a more personalized experience to your customers.

Conducting Market Research to Gain Valuable Insights

Market research is an essential tool in your marketing arsenal. It involves gathering and analyzing data about your industry, competitors, and target audience to make informed decisions. Through market research, you can gain insights into market trends, customer preferences, and competitive landscapes.

There are various research methods you can employ, such as surveys, focus groups, interviews, and data analysis. The key is to ask the right questions and listen to the needs and desires of your target audience. By keeping your finger on the pulse of the market, you can stay ahead of the curve and make strategic decisions that give your start-up a competitive edge.

Setting Clear Marketing Goals and Objectives

Every successful marketing strategy starts with clear goals and objectives. What do you want to achieve through your advertising efforts? Do you want to increase brand awareness? Drive more traffic to your website? Generate leads? Boost sales?

Setting Specific, Measurable, Attainable, Relevant, and time-bound (SMART) goals will help you stay focused and track your progress along the way. For example, a SMART goal could be to increase website traffic by 20% within the next three months. By having clear goals, you can align your advertising strategies and tactics accordingly.

Developing a Comprehensive Marketing Plan

Now that you have a solid understanding of marketing basics, it's time to create a comprehensive marketing plan. This plan will serve as your roadmap, outlining the overarching strategies and tactics you will use to achieve your marketing goals.

A marketing plan typically includes an executive summary, market analysis, target audience description, competitive analysis, positioning statement, goals and objectives, strategies, tactics, budget allocation, and a timeline. It's like a well-thought-out blueprint that keeps you on track and ensures that all your marketing efforts are coordinated and aligned.

The Role of Branding in Marketing Efforts

Branding is more than just a logo or a catchy tagline. It's the essence of your business and how you want to be perceived by your customers. A strong brand establishes trust, differentiates you from the competition, and creates emotional connections with your target audience.

CHAPTER 2: EMBRACING A CUSTOMER-CENTRIC APPROACH

Today, we're diving into the world of customer-centric marketing and how it can transform your advertising efforts into something truly remarkable.

Understanding the value of customer satisfaction and loyalty

In the fast-paced world of business, it's easy to get caught up in the numbers and lose sight of the most important element - the customer. In order to succeed, start-ups need to prioritize customer satisfaction and loyalty. Happy customers are not only more likely to continue doing business with you, but they also become your most powerful brand advocates.

Building strong customer relationships through effective communication

Effective communication is the foundation of any strong relationship, and it's no different when it comes to your customers. Take the time to really understand their needs and preferences, and then

tailor your communication accordingly. Whether it's through

emails, phone calls, or face-to-face interactions, make them feel heard, valued, and understood.

Creating a positive customer experience

Think about the last time you had an amazing customer experience - one that left you feeling wowed and excited to tell your friends about it. That's the kind of experience you need to create for your customers. From the moment they interact with your brand, every touchpoint should be designed to exceed their expectations and leave a lasting positive impression.

Implementing customer feedback and incorporating it into advertising strategies

Your customers are a goldmine of feedback, ideas, and insights. Make it a priority to actively seek feedback from them, whether through surveys, social media polls, or one-on-one conversations. This valuable feedback can then be incorporated into your advertising strategies, helping you create campaigns that truly resonate with your target audience.

Personalizing marketing messages and offers

Gone are the days of generic, one-size-fits-all marketing messages. In today's age of data and personalization, customers expect brands to understand their unique needs and deliver tailored experiences. Leverage the information you have about your customers to personalize your marketing messages, offers, and recommendations. By doing so, you'll create a deeper connection and increase the likelihood of conversion.

Leveraging technology to enhance customer interactions

Technology has revolutionized the way we interact with customers. From social media to chatbots and CRM systems, there are countless tools available to enhance and streamline customer interactions. Embrace these technologies and use them to your advantage. Automate repetitive tasks, provide quick and efficient customer support, and leverage data analytics to gain insights into customer behaviour.

Encouraging customer advocacy and referrals

Your customers can be your biggest cheerleaders, so don't be shy about asking for their support. Encourage them to share their positive experiences with their networks and reward them for their advocacy. Referral programs, exclusive discounts, or even just a heartfelt thank you can go a long way in fostering loyalty and driving new customers to your brand.

By embracing a customer-centric approach, you'll not only build stronger relationships with your customers but also create advertising campaigns that truly resonate with them

Your brand should reflect your start-up's values, personality, and unique selling proposition. It should be consistent across all your marketing channels, from your website to your social media profiles. By

investing in a strong and memorable brand, you can leave a lasting impression and build a loyal customer base.

The Importance of Tracking and Measuring Results

Last but not least, tracking and measuring the results of your marketing efforts is crucial. How do you know if your advertising campaigns are successful? Are you achieving your goals? Which channels are driving the most traffic or conversions?

By setting up proper tracking mechanisms and utilizing analytics tools, you can gather valuable data that tells you what's working and what's not. This data will help you make data-driven decisions, optimize your campaigns, and maximize your return on investment (ROI). Remember, marketing is a continuous process of learning and adapting, and data is your best friend in this journey.

CHAPTER 3: CRAFTING AN EFFECTIVE ADVERTISING STRATEGY

Ah, advertising. The glamorous side of marketing that often gets people excited and dreaming of big billboards and catchy jingles. But here's the thing - advertising is not just about creating eye-catching visuals or attention-grabbing slogans. It's about crafting a solid strategy that aligns with your overall marketing goals and reaches your target audience effectively. In this chapter, we're going to dive deep into the world of advertising and explore how to create an effective advertising strategy for your start-up.

Let's define what advertising is and its role in the broader marketing landscape. Advertising is a paid form of communication that promotes your products or services to a specific audience through various channels. It's one of the essential tools in your marketing toolbox, alongside other components like branding, public relations, and sales promotions. While advertising alone may not guarantee success, it plays a crucial role in building awareness, driving engagement, and ultimately converting prospects into customers.

Now that we have a clear understanding of advertising, let's talk about setting clear advertising objectives. Just like any other aspect of your business, your advertising efforts need to have a purpose. What do you want to achieve through your advertising? Is it to create brand awareness among a new target audience? Is it to drive traffic to your website or store? Or maybe it's to generate leads and increase sales? Whatever your objectives may be, it's essential to define them clearly before you dive into creating your advertising strategy. Without clear objectives, you'll be shooting in the dark, hoping something sticks.

Once your objectives are set, it's time to select the most suitable advertising channels to reach your target audience. This involves understanding your audience's media consumption habits, preferences, and demographics. Are they more active on social media platforms like Facebook and Instagram? Do they spend a significant amount of time watching videos on YouTube? Or are they more likely to be reached through traditional channels like television or radio? By understanding where your audience spends their time, you can strategically choose the channels that will give you the highest return on investment.

Now, let's talk about the content of your advertisements - the ad copy, visuals, and graphics. Your advertising materials need to be compelling, persuasive, and targeted to resonate with your audience. Gone are the days of one-size-fits-all ad campaigns. Today, personalization is key.

Tailor the messaging you use to speak directly to your audience's pain points, desires, and aspirations. Use language and visuals that resonate with them on an emotional level. Remember, the goal is to create an emotional connection with your audience, not to bombard them with a laundry list of features and benefits.

Speaking of visuals and graphics, don't underestimate their power in capturing attention and conveying your message. Humans are visual beings, and we are naturally drawn to visually appealing images. Invest in professional design or photography services to ensure that your visuals are top-notch. And don't forget to align your visuals with your brand identity. Consistency is key in building brand recognition and trust.

Now, let's talk about the advertising budget. Allocating your budget effectively is crucial to getting the most out of your advertising efforts. Start by setting a realistic budget based on your marketing objectives and overall business goals. There are multiple ways to determine your advertising budget - percentage of sales, competition-based, or objective and task method. Choose the one that aligns best with your business and industry. And remember, it's not about how much you spend, but how wisely you allocate your budget.

Last but not least, measuring and evaluating the success of your advertising campaigns is essential to ensure you are on the right track. Tracking key metrics and evaluating the return on investment will help you identify what works and what needs improvement. Utilize tools like Google Analytics, social media insights, or CRM systems to gather data and analyze the performance of your advertising campaigns. Based on these insights, make data-driven decisions and adjust your strategies accordingly.

Crafting an effective advertising strategy is a delicate balance of creativity, strategy, and data analysis. It's about understanding your audience, setting clear objectives, selecting the right channels, creating compelling content, allocating your budget wisely, and measuring your success. By following these steps and continuously refining your approach, you'll be well on your way to revamping your start-up's advertising strategies and dominating the market. So, get ready to unleash your inner marketing maverick and let your advertising efforts shine!

CHAPTER 4: UTILIZING TRADITIONAL ADVERTISING METHODS

Hey there, marketing mavericks! We've covered the basics of marketing, embraced a customer-centric approach, and crafted an effective advertising strategy. Now, it's time to dive into the world of traditional advertising methods. While digital advertising has taken centre stage in recent years, don't dismiss the power of tried-and-true techniques that have been around for decades.

You might be wondering, "Why should I bother with traditional advertising when digital seems to be the way to go?" Well, I'll let you in on a little secret. Traditional advertising methods still have their place in today's marketing landscape. They can complement your digital efforts and reach audiences that might not be as tuned in to the online world. So, let's explore some traditional advertising methods and discover how they can revamp your start-up's advertising strategies.

Print advertising is a classic way to get your message out there. Whether it's in newspapers or magazines, print ads provide a tangible experience for readers. There's something about flipping through a magazine and stumbling upon a beautifully designed ad that catches your eye. So, how can you leverage print advertising effectively?

First, let's talk about newspapers. Local newspapers have a strong presence in communities, making them an excellent avenue for reaching a specific target audience. If your start-up caters to a local market, placing an ad in the local newspaper can be a great way to generate awareness. Be sure to create compelling ad copy and use visuals that resonate with your target audience. Don't forget to consider the placement of your ad, as it can greatly impact its visibility and effectiveness.

Magazines, on the other hand, allow you to tap into specific niches and target more specialized audiences. For example, if you're in the fashion industry, advertising in a fashion magazine can put your brand in front of fashion-forward individuals who are passionate about the latest trends. Take the time to research and identify magazines that align with your target audience's interests and values.

Moving on to the airwaves, radio and television ads provide an opportunity to unleash the power of audio and visual storytelling. Radio ads, in particular, can be an affordable way to reach a wide audience. When creating a radio ad, focus on crafting a concise and memorable message that captures attention and drives action. Consider using humor or a catchy jingle to make your ad stand out from the rest.

Television ads, if budget allows, can be a game-changer. They offer the unique ability to combine visuals, audio, and storytelling to create a lasting impact. Use compelling visuals and a compelling narrative that resonates with your target audience. Consider partnering with a production company that specializes in creating high-quality commercials that leave a lasting impression.

Outdoor advertising, such as billboards and signage, allows you to literally take your message to the streets. Billboards, strategically placed along busy highways or in high-traffic areas, can generate widespread brand awareness. When designing a billboard, keep it simple, clear, and visually appealing. Avoid cluttering it with too much information or complex visuals that might be difficult to digest in a split second.

Direct mail campaigns might seem outdated in the digital age, but they can still be an effective way to grab attention and engage potential customers. A well-designed direct mail piece, personalized and targeted to the recipient's interests, can make a lasting impression. Consider incorporating special offers or discounts to entice recipients to take action. Just be sure to conduct thorough market research to ensure you're reaching the right audience with your direct mail campaign.

Another traditional advertising method worth exploring is cross-promotion with local businesses. Partnering with other businesses in your community can extend your reach and create mutually beneficial opportunities. For example, if you own a fitness apparel start-up, consider partnering with a local gym to offer exclusive discounts to their members. This collaboration not only exposes your brand to a new audience but also creates a sense of community and trust.

Now, here's the thing - traditional advertising methods shouldn't be considered in isolation. Instead, they should be part of an omnichannel advertising approach. Integrating traditional methods with your digital efforts can create a cohesive and powerful advertising strategy. For example, you can use a print ad as a call to action, directing readers to your website or social media platforms. Or you can leverage QR codes on billboards to drive traffic to specific landing pages or digital content.

So, don't underestimate the potential of traditional advertising methods. While digital advertising might be the star of the show, traditional methods still have their place in revamping your start-up's advertising strategies. Just remember, it's all about finding the right mix and balance between traditional and digital to reach your target audience and get the most out of your advertising efforts. Now go forth and make a splash with your traditional advertising initiatives, marketing mavericks!

CHAPTER 5: MAXIMIZING DIGITAL ADVERTISING OPPORTUNITIES

With the rise of the internet and technology, digital advertising has become an essential component of any advertising strategy. So, let's get started!

Understanding the importance of online presence and visibility

In today's digital age, having a strong online presence is crucial for your start-up's success. Consumers now turn to the internet to research products, compare prices, and make purchasing decisions. If your business doesn't have a solid online presence, you risk missing out on valuable opportunities to connect with your target audience.

To maximize your digital advertising efforts, it's essential to create a user-friendly website that is visually appealing and loaded with valuable content. Your website should reflect your brand's identity and effectively communicate your unique selling propositions. Additionally, optimizing your website for search engines (more on that later) will ensure that you're visible to potential customers who are actively looking for products or services like yours.

Exploring various digital advertising channels

The digital landscape offers endless possibilities when it comes to advertising channels. From search engine ads to social media ads, the options are aplenty. It's vital to understand the strengths and weaknesses of each channel to make informed decisions about where to allocate your advertising budget.

Google Ads, formerly known as Google AdWords, is one of the most popular online advertising platforms. By bidding on relevant keywords, you can have your ads displayed prominently in search engine results. This form of advertising allows you to target specific keywords, demographics, and locations, ensuring your ads reach the most relevant audience.

Another powerful digital advertising channel is social media. Platforms like Facebook, Instagram, Twitter, and LinkedIn offer robust advertising options to help you reach your target audience. By utilizing their advanced targeting capabilities, you can narrow down your audience based on demographics, interests, behaviour's, and more. Social media advertising allows for highly personalized and engaging ad experiences, increasing your chances of capturing attention and driving conversions.

Strategies for optimizing search engine marketing (SEM)

Search engine marketing (SEM) involves promoting your website by increasing its visibility in search engine results pages (SERPs) through paid advertising. As mentioned earlier, Google Ads plays a significant role in SEM. To optimize your SEM efforts, consider the following strategies:

1. Research and select the right keywords: Conduct thorough keyword research to identify the words and phrases your target audience is using to search for products or services like yours. By using the right keywords in your ad campaign, you can increase your chances of appearing in relevant search results.

2. Write compelling ad copy: Your ad copy should be concise, persuasive, and tailored to your target audience. Highlight the unique value propositions of your product or service and include a clear call-to-action that prompts users to take the desired action.

3. Landing page optimization: When users click on your ads, they should be directed to a relevant landing page that aligns with the ad's messaging. Optimize your landing pages to deliver a seamless user experience, ensuring that visitors find what they're looking for and are encouraged to convert.

Harnessing the potential of social media advertising

Social media has revolutionized the way we connect and engage with others, and it has also transformed the advertising landscape. Social media advertising offers unparalleled targeting capabilities, allowing you to deliver your message to the right people at the right time. Here are some strategies to make the most of social media advertising:

1. Define your target audience: Before launching any social media advertising campaign, take the time to define your target audience. Identify their demographics, interests, behaviours', and pain points. By understanding your audience, you can create highly relevant and engaging ad content.

2. Choose the right platform: Each social media platform attracts a different audience, so it's essential to choose the ones that align with your target audience. For example, if you're targeting professionals, LinkedIn might be a better choice than Instagram.

3. Create captivating content: Social media users are constantly bombarded with content, so it's crucial to create ads that stand out. Use eye-catching visuals, compelling headlines, and engaging

copy to capture attention and encourage users to take action.

Incorporating content marketing and storytelling in digital ads

In today's cluttered digital landscape, traditional advertising alone may not be enough to capture and retain your target audience's attention. Enter content marketing and storytelling. By incorporating these techniques into your digital ads, you can create a deeper connection with your audience.

Content marketing involves creating and distributing valuable and relevant content to attract and retain a clearly defined audience. Consider how you can provide helpful information, entertaining stories, or thought-provoking ideas in your digital ads. This approach positions your brand as an expert and builds trust with your audience.

Storytelling, on the other hand, taps into the power of narrative to engage and captivate your audience. Rather than simply promoting your product or service, tell a compelling story that connects with your target audience's emotions. Show them how your brand can make a positive impact on their lives.

Leveraging email marketing for targeted advertising

While email marketing may not be as flashy as some other digital advertising channels, it remains a highly effective way to reach and engage with your audience. Email marketing allows you to deliver personalized messages directly to each individual's inbox. Here's how you can leverage email marketing for targeted advertising:

1. Segment your email list: Divide your email list into smaller segments based on demographics, purchase behaviour, or engagement level. This segmentation allows you to send highly targeted and relevant ads to each segment, increasing the chances of conversion.

2. Craft enticing subject lines: The subject line is the gateway to your email. It should be compelling enough to entice recipients to open and read your message. Experiment with different subject lines and analyze the open rates to see what works best for your audience.

3. Personalize your messages: Personalization goes a long way in email marketing. Address recipients by their name and tailor the content of your emails to their preferences and interests. This personal touch makes your audience feel valued and increases the chances of conversion.

Mobile advertising strategies to cater to on-the-go consumers

In today's mobile-first world, it's essential to optimize your advertising strategies for mobile devices. With more people accessing the internet and engaging with content through their smartphones and tablets, mobile advertising offers significant opportunities to reach and connect with your audience. Consider the following strategies to make the most of mobile advertising:

1. Implement responsive design: Ensure that your website and digital ads are mobile-friendly and responsive across various devices and screen sizes. A seamless mobile experience is critical to capturing and retaining users' attention.

2. Utilize mobile-specific ad formats: Mobile advertising offers unique ad formats, such as interstitial ads, mobile banners, and in-app ads. Consider how these formats can enhance your advertising campaigns and engage your mobile audience effectively.

3. Location-based targeting: Take advantage of location-based targeting to deliver ads to users who are physically near your

business or in a specific geographical area. This strategy is particularly useful for driving foot traffic and targeting on-the-go consumers.

And there you have it - an overview of maximizing digital advertising opportunities for your start-up. By incorporating these strategies into your advertising efforts, you can tap into the vast potential of the digital landscape and reach your target audience effectively. Stay tuned for the next chapter, where we'll delve into the art of social media marketing.

CHAPTER 6: MAKING THE MOST OF SOCIAL MEDIA MARKETING

Social media has become an undeniable force in the advertising landscape. It's a platform that allows you to reach and engage with your target audience on a personal level, creating a strong brand presence and generating buzz around your product or service. In this chapter, we'll dive deep into the world of social media marketing and explore how you can harness its power to propel your start-up to new heights.

Social media platforms have revolutionized the way we communicate, connect, and consume content. They offer a unique opportunity for brands to directly interact with their audience, build brand loyalty, and boost brand awareness. With billions of active users across various social media channels, the potential reach and impact of social media marketing are unmatched. But how can you effectively tap into this power and make the most of it for your start-up? Let's find out.

First and foremost, it's crucial to understand the power and scope of different social media platforms. Each platform caters to a specific demographic and has its own nuances. Facebook, with its massive user base and diverse functionalities, is a must-have for most businesses. Instagram, known for its visual appeal and younger audience, is perfect for brands that rely heavily on visuals. Twitter, with its concise and real-time nature, is great for quick updates and engaging in conversations. LinkedIn, on the other hand, is the go-to platform for professional networking and B2B marketing. By identifying the right social media channels for your target audience, you can focus your efforts where they will yield the best results.

Creating a strong social media presence is paramount to your success. Your social media profiles should reflect your brand's personality and values, creating a consistent image across all platforms. Invest time in crafting compelling and shareable content that resonates with your audience. Think about what makes your start-up unique, and leverage that uniqueness to capture attention. Whether it's through informative blog posts, engaging videos, or eye-catching visuals, make sure your content is tailored to the preferences of your target audience. This will not only attract new followers but also encourage existing followers to share your content, expanding your reach organically.

Speaking of organic reach, user-generated content (UGC) and influencer marketing can be powerful tools in your social media marketing arsenal. User-generated content refers to content created by your customers or fans, such as reviews, testimonials, or user-submitted photos and videos. By incorporating UGC into your social media content, you not only strengthen your relationship with your customers but also amplify your brand's reach through their networks. Influencer marketing, on the other hand, involves partnering with popular social media personalities who have a significant following in your niche. By leveraging the influence of these influencers, you can reach a wider audience and build trust among your target market.

To ensure your social media marketing efforts are paying off, it's crucial to utilize social media analytics. Most social media platforms offer built-in analytics tools that provide valuable insights into the performance of your posts, engagement levels, and audience demographics. By regularly monitoring these metrics, you can gain a deeper understanding of what resonates with your audience and make data-driven decisions to optimize your content and approach. Don't be afraid to experiment and try new things based on the insights you gather. Social media is a dynamic landscape, and it's essential to adapt and evolve with changing trends and consumer behaviour's.

Building an active and loyal social media community is the ultimate goal of social media marketing. Engagement is key - make sure to actively interact with your followers, respond to their comments and messages, and make them feel valued. Encourage user-generated content, ask questions, and create opportunities for meaningful conversations. By fostering an active and positive community, you can tap into the power of word-of-mouth marketing, where your followers become brand advocates and spread the word about your start-up to their own networks.

In conclusion, social media marketing is an indispensable tool for any modern-day start-up. By understanding the power of social media platforms, creating a strong brand presence, and engaging with your audience in a meaningful way, you can leverage social media to boost brand awareness, drive traffic to your website, and ultimately, convert followers into loyal customers. So, go ahead and harness the power of social media marketing to revamp your start-up's advertising strategies and take your business to new heights!

CHAPTER 7: MASTERING THE ART OF SEARCH ENGINE OPTIMIZATION (SEO)

Hey there, marketing mavericks! In this chapter, we're going to dive headfirst into the wonderful world of search engine optimization (SEO). Now, I know what you're thinking - SEO sounds like a bunch of technical jargon that's best left to the experts. But fear not, my friends! I'm here to demystify this topic and show you how SEO can become your secret weapon in revamping your start-up's advertising strategies.

So, let's start with the basics. SEO, in simple terms, is the practice of optimizing your website and its content to rank higher in search engine results. Why does it matter? Well, think about it - when was the last time you went beyond the first page of search results? Exactly. The higher you rank, the more visibility your website gets, and the more traffic and potential customers you'll attract. It's like having your own personal billboard on the internet highway.

The first step in mastering SEO is conducting keyword research. Keywords are the words or phrases that people type into search engines when looking for information. By understanding what your target audience is searching for, you can optimize your website content to match their queries. There are plenty of tools out there to help you with keyword research, such as Google's Keyword Planner or SEMrush. Get in the mind of your customers and think about what they would type into that search bar.

Once you've identified your keywords, it's time to put them to good use. Incorporate them naturally into your website's content, including your page titles, headings, and body text. But be careful not to overdo it - search engines are smart and can sniff out keyword stuffing. Remember, the goal is to provide valuable and relevant content to your audience.

Now, here's a golden tip for you - backlinks. Backlinks are like little endorsements from other websites, telling search engines that your content is trustworthy and relevant. The more quality backlinks you have, the better your chances of ranking higher. So, how do you get these backlinks? Well, it's not easy, but it's worth the effort. Build relationships within your industry or niche and reach out to other website owners, asking them to link to your content. Guest blogging is another great way to earn backlinks while showcasing your expertise.

Speaking of expertise, if you have a local business, don't forget to leverage local SEO techniques. Optimizing your website for local searches can make a huge difference in attracting customers within your specific region. Make sure your contact information, address, and hours of operation are clear and consistent across all online platforms. Register your business on Google My Business and other local directories. Encourage your happy customers to leave reviews, as they can also boost your local ranking.

Now, I need to give you a word of caution - SEO is not a one-time thing. Search engines constantly update their algorithms, which means you need to stay on your toes. What worked yesterday might not work tomorrow. Stay up to date with industry trends, follow reputable SEO blogs, and keep experimenting. Pay attention to your analytics and track your SEO progress using tools like Google Analytics. They'll show you what's working and what's not so you can make informed adjustments.

Remember, my fellow mavericks, mastering SEO takes time and patience. It's a long-term investment in your start-up's online presence. So, keep tinkering, keep optimizing, and never stop learning. Before you know it, you'll be climbing those search engine rankings and attracting a steady stream of qualified traffic to your website.

Phew! That was a lot to cover, but I hope you're feeling empowered and ready to tackle the world of SEO. In the next chapter, we'll explore the power of content marketing and how it can take your advertising strategies to new heights. Until then, keep optimizing and stay maverick!

CHAPTER 8: HARNESSING THE POWER OF CONTENT MARKETING

Let's define what content marketing is and why it's important for your start-up. Simply put, content marketing is all about creating valuable and informative content that resonates with your target audience. It's not about promoting your products or services directly, but rather establishing your brand as a trusted authority in your industry.

Why is content marketing important? Well, think about it. In today's digital age, consumers are bombarded with advertisements everywhere they turn. Traditional advertising methods are

becoming less effective, and customers are craving something more authentic and meaningful. That's where content marketing comes in. It allows you to connect with your audience on a deeper level by providing them with valuable information, insights, and solutions to their problems.

Now, let's talk about creating high-quality and valuable content. Remember, content is king! Your content should be informative, engaging, and tailored to your target audience's needs and interests. Whether it's blog posts, infographics, videos, or podcasts, you need to ensure that your content is well-written, visually appealing, and easily digestible.

But it's not just about creating amazing content; you also need to optimize it for search engines and keywords. Research and identify relevant keywords that your audience is searching for and incorporate them naturally into your content. This will help your content rank higher in search engine results and attract organic traffic to your website.

Speaking of attracting traffic, let's talk about distributing your content. Don't just limit yourself to one channel. Explore various distribution channels such as your website, social media platforms, email newsletters, and even industry publications. The more channels you utilize, the greater your reach and the more opportunities you have to connect with your audience.

Now, let's get creative! To truly stand out in the crowded digital landscape, you need to engage with your audience through storytelling and unique perspectives. Don't be afraid to inject your brand's personality and values into your content. Tell stories that resonate with your audience, evoke emotions, and leave a lasting impression.

Of course, your content marketing efforts won't mean much if you can't measure their impact. That's why it's crucial to track and measure the results of your content marketing initiatives. Set clear goals and key performance indicators (KPIs) such as website traffic, social media engagement, lead generation, and conversion rates. This data will provide valuable insights into what's working and what's not, allowing you to make informed decisions and optimize your content marketing strategies.

Lastly, let's talk about ROI. Yes, content marketing may not give you an immediate ROI like traditional advertising methods, but it's a long-term investment in your brand's reputation and customer loyalty. Remember, content marketing is about building trust and establishing your brand as an industry thought leader. The ROI may not be immediate, but the long-term benefits are priceless.

Content marketing is a powerful tool that can take your advertising efforts to new heights. By creating valuable content, optimizing it for search engines, distributing it through various channels, and measuring its impact, you'll be on your way to becoming a content marketing maverick!

Keep up the great work, my fellow marketing mavericks, and I'll see you in the next chapter as we explore the exciting world of influencer marketing. Stay tuned!

CHAPTER 9: IMPLEMENTING INFLUENCER MARKETING STRATEGIES

Influencer marketing has become a game-changer for advertising, allowing businesses to reach their target audience in a more authentic and engaging way. So, let's jump right in!

First off, let's understand the concept and benefits of influencer marketing. Influencers are individuals who have built a loyal following and possess the power to influence the purchasing decisions of their audience. By partnering with influencers, your start-up can tap into their engaged community and expand your reach.

Identifying relevant influencers within your industry or niche is the first step. Look for influencers whose values align with your brand and whose audience matches your target market. Remember, it's not all about follower count; it's about finding influencers who have an engaged and loyal following.

Building relationships and partnerships with influencers is crucial. Approach them with a personalized outreach and show genuine interest in their work. Remember, influencers are people too! It's important to nurture these relationships and create mutual trust and respect.

Collaborating on sponsored content or endorsements is one way to work with influencers. Keep in mind that transparency is key. Clearly define the expectations, deliverables, and compensation involved in the collaboration. Authenticity is crucial, so give influencers creative freedom to maintain their unique voice and style, while also aligning with your brand's objectives.

Setting clear objectives and expectations in influencer campaigns is essential. Whether you're looking to increase brand awareness, drive website traffic, or boost sales, establish measurable goals before launching the campaign. This will help you track the success and impact of your influencer marketing efforts.

Measuring the success of influencer marketing isn't always straightforward. While traditional metrics like reach, engagement, and conversions are important, keep in mind that the value of influencer marketing goes beyond direct sales. Look for long-term relationships, increased brand affinity, and a positive brand image within the influencer's community.

Of course, like any advertising strategy, influencer marketing also comes with its challenges. It's important to avoid common pitfalls such as partnering with influencers whose values don't align with your brand or relying solely on influencer popularity without considering audience engagement. Be sure to choose influencers whose audience genuinely connects with your brand.

So, there you have it, influencer marketing in a nutshell. It's an exciting opportunity for start-ups to tap into the power of social influence and connect with their target audience in a more personal way. Just remember, authenticity and relationship-building are key to successful influencer marketing campaigns.

Now that you've explored the world of influencer marketing, get ready for Chapter 10 where we'll uncover the power of video marketing and how it can take your advertising efforts to the next level. See you there!

CHAPTER 10: TAPPING INTO THE POWER OF VIDEO MARKETING

Video marketing has skyrocketed in popularity in recent years, and it's easy to see why. People love watching videos - whether it's short clips on social media or longer, informative content. Videos have a unique ability to capture attention, evoke emotions, and deliver messages in a powerful and engaging way. If you want your advertising to make a lasting impact, incorporating video should be high on your priority list.

Now, you might be thinking, "But I'm a start-up on a budget. Can I actually afford to create videos?" Absolutely! The rise of affordable video production tools, such as smartphones and editing software, has made it easier than ever to create professional-looking videos on a shoestring budget. So don't let cost deter you from exploring this valuable avenue.

One of the first things you need to consider when diving into video marketing is the suitable format for your advertising goals. Are you looking to create product demos, customer testimonials, or perhaps explainer videos? Each format serves a different purpose, so be sure to tailor your video content to your specific objectives.

Next, it's time to put your creative hat on and start brainstorming ideas for your videos. Remember, the key is to grab your viewers' attention from the very beginning and keep them engaged until the end. Incorporate storytelling and emotions to make a lasting impact. Whether you're tugging at heartstrings or tickling funny bones, make sure your videos connect with your audience on a deeper level.When it comes to optimizing your videos for search engines and social media platforms, keywords are your best friends. Conduct keyword research to uncover the terms your target audience is searching for, and then incorporate them strategically throughout your video titles, descriptions, and tags. This will increase the chances of your videos being discovered by the right people.

Now that you've created your videos, it's time to share them with the world. Utilize various channels to distribute your content, including your website, social media platforms, and YouTube. Don't forget to optimize your videos for each platform by resizing them and including captions or subtitles if necessary. The more visibility your videos have, the greater the impact they'll have on your advertising efforts.

Speaking of impact, storytelling and emotions are incredibly powerful tools in video marketing. Craft a compelling narrative that resonates with your audience and sparks an emotional response. Whether you're making them laugh, cry, or feel inspired, striking an emotional chord will make your videos memorable and shareable.

Of course, once you've launched your video campaigns, it's essential to analyze their success and adjust your strategies accordingly. Pay attention to video metrics such as views, engagement, and shares to gauge how well your videos are performing. Use this data to fine-tune your future video marketing efforts and double down on what's working.

Remember that video marketing is a dynamic field that continues to evolve. Stay on top of emerging trends and technologies in the video marketing landscape, such as augmented reality (AR) and virtual reality (VR). Don't be afraid to experiment with innovative ideas and embrace new forms of interactive content. The more agile and adaptable you are, the more successful your video marketing initiatives will be.

I hope you're now equipped with a solid understanding of video marketing and the powerful impact it can have on your advertising strategies. So, grab your camera and start unleashing your creativity. Lights, camera, action!

CHAPTER 11: NURTURING A POSITIVE ONLINE REPUTATION

Imagine this - you're considering buying a new product or trying out a new service. What's the first thing you do? If you're like most people, you turn to the almighty power of the internet and start researching. And what you read online, the reviews, the comments, they heavily influence your decision-making process.

That's why managing your online reputation is crucial. Your reputation is your most valuable asset in today's digital world. It can make or break your business. So, let's dive right in and explore some strategies to ensure that your online reputation is in tip-top shape.

First and foremost, you need to understand the importance of online reputation management. Many start-ups underestimate how vital it is to actively monitor and respond to customer reviews and feedback. Your customers will leave reviews whether you ask for them or not. By actively engaging with your online audience, you have an opportunity to address any concerns, resolve issues, and showcase your commitment to customer satisfaction.

When it comes to building a positive brand image through proactive communication, authenticity is key. Be transparent and genuine in your interactions. If a customer expresses dissatisfaction, respond promptly and professionally. Offer a sincere apology if there was a mistake on your part, and propose a solution to rectify the situation. By taking these measures, you demonstrate your dedication to customer care, which will reflect positively on your online reputation.

Now, let's talk about the elephant in the room - negative comments and criticisms. It's inevitable that at some point, you'll encounter them. When you do, it's crucial to adopt a level-headed approach. Take a step back and assess the situation objectively. Avoid getting defensive or engaging in arguments online. Instead, respond calmly, address the concerns, and try to find a resolution privately. Remember, other potential customers are observing your response, and how you handle the situation will speak volumes about your company's values.

On the flip side, positive reviews and testimonials are golden opportunities to showcase your brand's worth. Leverage these positive experiences in your advertising efforts. Feature them on your website, social media platforms, or even transform them into compelling video testimonials. These testimonials add credibility and act as social proof, influencing potential customers to trust and choose your brand.

Managing your online reputation goes beyond monitoring and responding. It's about creating a culture that values customer satisfaction and actively encourages happy customers to spread the word. Encourage satisfied customers to leave reviews and testimonials, and express your gratitude for their support. Word of mouth is a powerful advertising tool, and positive online reviews are the modern-day equivalent of it.

To effectively manage your online reputation, there are a plethora of tools and platforms available. Online reputation management tools such as Google Alerts, Mention, or Brand24 can help you monitor online mentions of your brand and track sentiment. Social media listening tools like Hootsuite or Sprout Social can provide insights into customer conversations and sentiment on various social media platforms. These tools allow you to stay on top of what people are saying about your brand, enabling you to respond promptly and appropriately.

Ultimately, nurturing a positive online reputation is an ongoing process. It requires constant vigilance and a commitment to maintaining open lines of communication with your customers. By actively engaging with your audience, addressing concerns, and leveraging positive experiences, you can build a strong online reputation that attracts and retains customers.

Remember, in today's digital age, your online reputation is paramount. It's the first impression potential customers have of your business, and it influences their purchasing decisions. So, take the time to nurture and protect your online reputation - it's an investment that will pay off in the long run.

Now that we've explored the ins and outs of nurturing a positive online reputation, let's move on to the next chapter, where we'll harness the power of data and analytics for advertising insights. Stay tuned, my marketing mavericks, there's still plenty more to discover!

CHAPTER 12: HARNESSING DATA AND ANALYTICS FOR ADVERTISING INSIGHTS

Nowadays, data is everything. From what people search online to their purchasing behaviour, we have access to a plethora of information that can help us make informed decisions about our advertising strategies. But before we jump into the nitty-gritty, let's take a moment to understand why data and analytics are so important.

Data and analytics allow us to move beyond guesswork. By analyzing patterns, trends, and consumer behaviour, we can better understand our target audience and tailor our advertising messages to resonate with them. It's like having a secret decoder ring that unlocks the mysteries of what makes your customers tick.

The first step in harnessing data and analytics is collecting the right information. Depending on your industry and advertising channels, this can include data from website analytics, social media insights, customer surveys, and even sales numbers. The key is to have a system in place that captures and compiles this data effectively.

Once you have the data in hand, it's time to analyze it. This is where tools like Google Analytics, customer relationship management (CRM) systems, and marketing automation software come into play. These tools can help you crunch the numbers and identify patterns that will inform your advertising decisions.

One powerful technique you can use is A/B testing or split testing. Essentially, you create two variations of an ad or landing page and compare their performance. By testing different elements such as headlines, visuals, or calls to action, you can see which version resonates better with your audience. This iterative approach allows you to optimize your advertising strategies over time.

Tracking key performance indicators (KPIs) is another crucial aspect of data analysis. These metrics serve as benchmarks to measure the success of your advertising campaigns. Depending on your goals, KPIs can include click-through rates (CTR), conversion rates, customer acquisition cost (CAC), or return on advertising spend (ROAS). Tracking these metrics can help you identify what's working and what needs improvement.

To make the most of your data, consider utilizing marketing automation and CRM systems. These tools can provide valuable insights into customer behaviour, segment your audience, and even automate certain aspects of your advertising campaigns. By integrating these systems into your overall marketing stack, you can streamline operations and make data-driven decisions.

Now, I know all this talk about data and analytics can seem overwhelming, especially for start-ups with limited resources. But fear not, my marketing mavericks! There are plenty of simple and cost-effective ways to get started. Google Analytics, for instance, is a free tool that provides valuable insights into your website traffic and audience demographics.

Lastly, visualizing your data can make it easier to understand and communicate your findings. Create dashboards and reports that compile relevant data into easy-to-understand visualizations. These visuals can help you identify trends, communicate insights to stakeholders, and make data-driven decisions more effectively.

By collecting and analyzing the right data, testing and tracking your advertising efforts, and utilizing tools like marketing automation and CRM systems, you can make informed decisions that will supercharge your advertising strategies.

Remember, data is your secret weapon in the ever-evolving advertising landscape. So, go forth, my marketing mavericks, and let data guide you on the path to advertising success!

CHAPTER 13:
STAYING AHEAD
WITH INNOVATIVE
ADVERTISING
TECHNIQUES

We live in a world that is constantly evolving, and advertising is no exception. To truly revamp your start-up's advertising strategies, it is essential to stay ahead of the game and embrace the latest innovative techniques. In this chapter, we will explore some of the emerging trends and technologies in advertising that can give your brand a competitive edge.

One of the most exciting developments in advertising is the integration of augmented reality (AR) and virtual reality (VR) experiences. AR and VR have the power to transport customers into immersive and interactive worlds, allowing them to engage with your brand on a whole new level. Whether it's through AR filters on social media platforms or VR experiences at events or pop-up stores, these technologies provide a unique and memorable way to advertise your products or services.

Artificial intelligence (AI) is another game-changer in the advertising industry. With AI, you can personalize your advertising messages and offers based on individual customer preferences and behaviour. By harnessing the power of AI, you can create targeted marketing campaigns that resonate with your audience on a deeper level. Chatbots powered by AI can also enhance customer interactions, providing instant and personalized assistance to potential customers.

Conversational marketing is another innovative technique that can revolutionize your advertising efforts. By engaging in real-time conversations with customers, whether it's through chatbots, social media messaging, or live chat on your website, you can gather valuable insights about their needs and preferences. Conversational marketing allows you to build meaningful relationships with your customers, establishing trust and loyalty that can translate into long-term success.

Gamification is a fun and interactive way to engage with your audience and promote your brand. By incorporating gaming elements into your advertising campaigns, you can create a sense of excitement and competition that motivates your customers to interact with your brand. From quizzes and contests to interactive mobile apps, gamification can be a powerful tool for capturing attention and driving customer engagement.

Influencer collaborations and user-generated content campaigns have become increasingly popular in recent years. Partnering with influencers who have a strong presence in your target market can help you tap into their loyal following and leverage their credibility and trust. User-generated content, on the other hand, allows your customers to become brand advocates and share their own experiences with your products or services. Both influencer collaborations and user-generated content can help you reach a wider audience and build a strong community around your brand.

As a start-up, it is crucial to stay informed and agile when it comes to advertising innovations. Keep an eye on industry trends, attend conferences and workshops, and stay connected with other marketing professionals to ensure that you are up to date with the latest developments. The advertising landscape is constantly evolving, so it's important to be open to new ideas and willing to adapt your strategies as needed.

By embracing innovative advertising techniques, you can give your start-up a competitive edge and captivate your target audience in new and exciting ways. Whether it's through augmented reality, artificial intelligence, conversational marketing, gamification, or influencer collaborations, the possibilities are endless. Stay ahead of the curve and be a marketing maverick by embracing the power of innovation in your advertising strategies.

CHAPTER 14: BUILDING STRATEGIC PARTNERSHIPS FOR EFFECTIVE ADVERTISING

In the ever-evolving world of marketing and advertising, it's essential for startups to think outside the box and explore new avenues for reaching their target audience. One powerful strategy that can significantly enhance advertising efforts is building strategic partnerships. By partnering with other businesses or organizations, startups can leverage each other's resources, expertise, and networks to maximize their advertising impact. In this chapter, we will delve into the benefits of strategic partnerships and provide practical insights on how to build and capitalize on these alliances.

Understanding the benefits of strategic partnerships in advertising:

Strategic partnerships offer numerous advantages for startups looking to revamp their advertising strategies. Firstly, these partnerships provide access to a wider audience. By collaborating with a complementary business or organization, startups can tap into their partner's existing customer base, gaining exposure to a whole new set of potential customers. This increased reach ensures that advertising efforts are more targeted and cost-effective.

Secondly, strategic partnerships offer enhanced credibility and trust. By associating with a reputable partner, startups can borrow some of their partner's established brand equity, instantly gaining credibility in the eyes of their target audience. This trust factor can greatly influence consumer behaviour and increase the likelihood of conversions.

Lastly, strategic partnerships provide access to shared resources and expertise. Startups can pool their marketing budgets with their partners, allowing for the execution of larger-scale advertising campaigns that would otherwise be unattainable individually. Additionally, partners can bring complementary skills and knowledge to the table, resulting in a more robust and comprehensive advertising strategy.

Identifying potential partners within the industry or related sectors:

The first step in building strategic partnerships is to identify potential partners within the industry or related sectors. Startups should seek out businesses or organizations that share their target audience and have complementary products or services. For example, a fitness apparel startup could consider partnering with a local gym or a health food store. It's crucial to ensure that the partnership makes sense from both a logical and strategic standpoint.

Creating mutually beneficial collaboration opportunities:

Once potential partners have been identified, startups should reach out and explore collaboration opportunities. It's essential to approach the partnership with a mindset of creating mutual benefits. This means identifying ways in which both parties can gain value. For example, a mutual benefit could be increased brand exposure for both partners through joint advertising campaigns.

Collaboration opportunities can take various forms, such as co-branding initiatives, co-marketing campaigns, or joint events. Startups should be open to brainstorming ideas with their potential partners and finding innovative ways to collaborate. The key is to create a win-win situation where both parties can leverage the alliance to achieve their advertising objectives.

Exploring co-branding and co-marketing initiatives:

Co-branding initiatives involve the joint creation and promotion of a product or service by two or more brands. By collaborating on a co-branded offering, startups can combine their resources, expertise, and customer bases to create a more compelling and differentiated product. This collaboration not only saves costs but also creates a unique value proposition that appeals to both sets of customers.

Co-marketing campaigns, on the other hand, involve joint marketing efforts by two or more brands. This could include cross-promotion on social media, sharing advertising space, or even hosting joint webinars or workshops. Co-marketing allows startups to reach a wider audience and leverage each other's brand equity, resulting in increased visibility and credibility for both parties.

Cross-promoting with partners through various channels:

Cross-promotion is an effective way to amplify advertising efforts. By collaborating with partners, startups can strategically leverage each other's marketing channels. This could include guest blogging on each other's websites, featuring partner content in newsletters, or promoting each other on social media. Cross-promotion allows startups to tap into their partner's existing audience, widening their reach and increasing brand exposure.

Sharing resources and expertise to enhance advertising efforts:

One of the most valuable aspects of strategic partnerships is the sharing of resources and expertise. Startups can collaborate with partners to pool marketing budgets, enabling them to execute more

impactful and far-reaching advertising campaigns. This shared financial burden reduces individual costs and allows for more extensive advertising initiatives.

Moreover, strategic partnerships provide an opportunity for startups to tap into their partner's knowledge and skills. This can include access to specialized marketing expertise, advanced technology platforms, or creative resources that can enhance and elevate advertising strategies. By leveraging each other's strengths and resources, startups can achieve more significant advertising results.

Measuring the impact and success of partnership campaigns:

As with any advertising initiative, measuring the impact and success of partnership campaigns is crucial. Startups should establish clear metrics and KPIs to track the effectiveness of their collaborative efforts. This could include measuring the increase in brand awareness, lead generation, customer engagement, or even sales conversions.

Collecting and analyzing data on the campaign's performance will provide insights into its effectiveness, enabling startups to make data-driven decisions for future partnership campaigns. It's essential to regularly assess and refine strategies based on these insights to ensure ongoing success.

Building strategic partnerships is a powerful and often underutilized strategy for startups looking to revamp their advertising strategies. By collaborating with complementary businesses or organizations, startups can leverage each other's resources, reach a wider audience, enhance credibility, and access shared expertise. Through co-branding, co-marketing, cross-promotion, and resource sharing, startups can maximize their advertising impact and achieve long-term success. It's essential for startups to recognize the value of strategic partnerships and embrace these alliances to stay competitive in the dynamic landscape of advertising.

CHAPTER 15: EFFECTIVE EVENT MARKETING STRATEGIES

Events can be incredibly powerful for advertising and brand building, as they offer a unique opportunity to connect with your target audience in a more personal and immersive way.

Understanding the Role of Events in Advertising and Brand Building

Events have the power to create a memorable and lasting impression on your audience. Whether it's a trade show, conference, workshop, or even a local community event, each offers a chance to showcase your brand, products, or services in an interactive and engaging way. Events allow you to bring your brand to life and connect with potential customers on a deeper level. They provide an opportunity to tell your brand story, demonstrate your expertise, and build credibility within your industry.

Identifying Suitable Events to Reach the Target Audience

When it comes to event marketing, it's important to choose events that align with your target audience and business objectives. Consider the demographics, interests, and behaviours of your ideal customers. Are they likely to attend trade shows or industry conferences? Or would they be more interested in local community events or workshops? By understanding your audience, you can identify the events where you are most likely to make a meaningful impact and reach potential customers who are already interested in what you have to offer.

Creating Engaging and Memorable Event Experiences

Once you've identified the right events to participate in, it's time to plan out your event strategy. This is where creativity, innovation, and out-of-the-box thinking come into play. Think about how you can differentiate yourself from other participants and create a memorable experience for attendees. Consider interactive demonstrations, product launches, gamification elements, or even live performances. The key is to make sure your event booth or presentation stands out and leaves a lasting impression.

Utilizing Event Sponsorship and Branding Opportunities

Events often offer various sponsorship and branding opportunities that can enhance your visibility and credibility. Consider becoming a sponsor for the event or securing speaking opportunities. This will allow you to position yourself as an industry expert and gain credibility in front of a captive audience. Additionally, make use of banners, signage, and branded giveaways to ensure your brand is visible throughout the event venue.

Incorporating Social - Media and Digital Channels in Event Marketing

It's crucial to leverage social media and other digital channels to amplify your event marketing efforts. Create buzz before the event by sharing teasers, behind-the-scenes content, and event updates on social media. Encourage attendees to share their experiences using event-specific hashtags. During the event, live-stream presentations or share real-time updates to engage a wider audience who couldn't be present physically. After the event, continue the conversation online by sharing highlights, photos, and testimonials from attendees.

Measuring Event Success and ROI through Various Metrics

As with any marketing initiative, it's important to measure the success and return on investment (ROI) of your event marketing efforts. Establish clear goals and set key performance indicators (KPIs) to track and evaluate your event's impact. Monitor metrics such as the number of leads generated, social media engagement, website traffic, brand mentions, or even direct sales resulting from the event. These will help you gauge the success of your event and identify areas for improvement in future events.

Leveraging Post-Event Activities for Ongoing Advertising Opportunities

Don't let the momentum from your event die down after it's over. Post-event activities are just as important in maximizing the impact of your event marketing efforts. Follow up with attendees through personalized emails or messages, thanking them for their participation and offering any special promotions or incentives. Leverage testimonials or reviews from satisfied attendees to build social proof and attract future customers. Additionally, utilize the content generated during the event, such as photos or videos, to create engaging social media posts or blog articles that continue to promote your brand and capture the attention of a wider audience.

Event marketing provides a unique opportunity to create meaningful connections with your target audience and boost your brand's visibility. By choosing the right events, creating engaging experiences, utilizing branding opportunities, and leveraging digital channels, you can make your events a cornerstone of your advertising strategy. Remember to measure the impact of your events and use post-event activities to fuel ongoing advertising opportunities. So go ahead, embrace event marketing, and let your creativity shine!

That's it for Chapter 15, my marketing mavericks! In the next chapter, we'll be exploring the exciting world of guerrilla marketing tactics. Get ready to think outside the box and unleash your unconventional side. Until then, keep daring to be different and never stop exploring new ways to revamp your start-up's advertising strategies.

CHAPTER 16: IMPLEMENTING GUERRILLA MARKETING TACTICS

Now, you might be wondering, what exactly is guerrilla marketing? Well, it's all about thinking outside the box and using unconventional methods to grab attention and create memorable experiences for your audience. Guerrilla marketing is all about being bold, creative, and surprising in your advertising efforts.

One of the key advantages of guerrilla marketing is that it doesn't require a huge budget. In fact, some of the most effective guerrilla marketing campaigns have been executed on a shoestring budget. So, let's explore some creative and low-cost guerrilla marketing ideas that can give your start-up a significant boost.

First up, let's talk about street art. You've probably seen those eye-catching and thought-provoking murals painted on the sides of buildings or underpasses. Well, street art can be a powerful tool for guerrilla marketing. By collaborating with local artists, you can create unique and captivating artworks that tell your brand's story or promote your products. These murals can become landmarks in your community and generate buzz around your start-up.

Another guerrilla marketing tactic that has gained popularity is the flash mob. Now, I know what you're thinking - aren't flash mobs a thing of the past? Well, not quite! If done right, a well-organized flash mob can create a viral sensation and generate tremendous exposure for your brand. Whether it's a surprise dance routine in a crowded public space or a coordinated event with a specific theme, a flash mob can capture the attention of passersby and create a memorable experience that they won't forget anytime soon.

But guerrilla marketing isn't just about street art and flash mobs. It can take many forms depending on your creativity and the nature of your business. For example, you can create pop-up stores or installations in unexpected locations to showcase your products and engage with potential customers. These pop-up experiences allow you to interact directly with your target audience and create a sense of exclusivity and urgency around your brand.

Social media can be a powerful tool to amplify your guerrilla marketing campaigns. By capturing videos or photos of your guerrilla efforts and sharing them on social media platforms, you can reach a wider audience and generate organic buzz. Just imagine the potential impact of a well-executed guerrilla marketing campaign going viral on Instagram or Twitter or whatever name they change it too!

Now, before you dive headfirst into the world of guerrilla marketing, there are a few things you need to keep in mind. Firstly, while being bold and creative is essential, it's important to ensure that your guerrilla marketing tactics are legal and ethical. So, make sure you research local regulations and obtain any necessary permits before executing your campaign.

Secondly, remember that guerrilla marketing is all about creating a memorable experience for your audience. So, focus on quality rather than quantity. One impactful guerrilla marketing campaign can have a far greater impact than several lacklustre ones. So, invest time and effort in brainstorming ideas that truly resonate with your target audience.

Lastly, always measure the impact and effectiveness of your guerrilla marketing efforts. This way, you can identify what worked well and what didn't, allowing you to refine your future campaigns. You can track metrics such as social media engagement, website traffic, and sales to determine the success of your guerrilla marketing initiatives.

There you have it - a glimpse into the world of guerrilla marketing. By embracing unconventional and creative tactics, you can captivate your audience, generate buzz around your start-up, and make a lasting impression. So go ahead, think outside the box, and let your creativity run wild!

Remember, being a marketing maverick means taking risks, pushing boundaries, and embracing the unexpected. So, get out there and make some noise with your guerrilla marketing tactics. Your start-up is ready to be the talk of the town!

CHAPTER 17: BUILDING A STRONG ONLINE COMMUNITY

Now that we've explored various advertising strategies and channels, it's time to dive into the importance of building a strong online community for your start-up. In today's digital age, where people spend more time connecting online than ever before, having a loyal and engaged community can be a game-changer for your advertising efforts.

So, what exactly is an online community? It's a group of like-minded individuals who come together virtually to share common interests, ideas, and values. Building an online community allows your start-up to connect with your target audience on a deeper level, foster relationships, and create brand advocates. Let's delve into why and how you can build an online community that enhances your advertising strategies.

Understanding the value of online communities for advertising

An online community offers several advantages for your advertising efforts. Firstly, it provides a platform for direct interaction with your target audience. This means you can gain valuable insights, tailor your messaging, and refine your advertising campaigns based on real-time feedback. Additionally, a strong online community creates a sense of belonging and loyalty among members, making them more likely to engage with and share your advertising content.

Creating a community around the brand or industry niche

To build an online community, you need to establish a common thread that brings people together. This can be cantered around your brand's values, a specific industry niche, or a shared interest. For example, if your start-up sells eco-friendly products, you can create a community around sustainable living and environmental activism. By aligning your community with something meaningful and relevant, you attract individuals who are genuinely interested in what you have to offer.

Engaging with community members through content and discussion

Once you've identified your community, it's essential to engage with its members through compelling content and meaningful discussions. Share valuable information and resources that align with their interests and values. Encourage conversation and feedback, and actively participate in discussions. Show genuine interest in what community members have to say, and make them feel heard and valued.

Building trust and loyalty within the online community

Trust is the foundation of any community. To build trust, it's important to be transparent, authentic, and consistent in your interactions with community members. Be honest about your start-up's journey, share behind-the-scenes glimpses, and respond to inquiries promptly. By building trust and fostering a sense of belonging, you cultivate loyalty within your community, which translates into loyal customers who will advocate for your brand.

Leveraging user-generated content and testimonials from the community

User-generated content is a powerful tool when it comes to advertising. Encourage community members to create and share content related to your brand. This can be in the form of reviews, testimonials, blog posts, videos, or social media posts. By showcasing user-generated content, you not only leverage the creativity and passion of your community, but you also build social proof, which is crucial for attracting new customers.

Encouraging advocacy and word-of-mouth referrals within the community

An engaged and loyal community is more likely to advocate for your brand. Encourage community members to share their positive experiences with your start-up, both online and offline. Offer incentives for referrals or testimonials. Word-of-mouth referrals from community members carry more weight than traditional advertising because they come from trusted sources.

Measuring community growth, engagement, and impact on advertising

To evaluate the success of your community-building efforts, it's important to measure community growth and engagement. Track metrics such as the number of community members, participation in discussions, content creation, and referrals. Additionally, assess how your community impacts your advertising campaigns. Are community members more likely to engage with your ads? Do they generate more sales? Analyzing these metrics will help you understand the ROI of building an online community and make informed decisions about your advertising strategies moving forward.

Building a strong online community takes time, effort, and a genuine commitment to connecting with your target audience. However, the benefits are worth it. By investing in community building, you cultivate a loyal customer base, gain valuable insights, and create brand advocates who will amplify your advertising efforts. So, start building that online community today and watch your advertising strategies soar to new heights!

CHAPTER 18: EMBRACING SUSTAINABILITY IN ADVERTISING

You may be wondering, why should sustainability even matter in advertising? Well, the truth is that today's consumers are more conscious about the environment and social issues than ever before. They want to see brands that align with their values and take a stand on important matters. By embracing sustainability in your advertising efforts, you not only appeal to these conscious consumers but also contribute to a better, greener world.

So, how can you incorporate sustainability messaging in your advertising? It's all about being authentic and genuine. Don't just greenwash your way to success by slapping a few eco-friendly claims on your ads. Instead, take a holistic approach by incorporating sustainability into the very fabric of your brand.

Start by highlighting your eco-friendly and socially responsible initiatives. If your products are made from recycled materials or if you're using renewable energy in your manufacturing process, shout it from the rooftops! Show your audience that you care about the planet and are taking concrete steps to reduce your environmental footprint.

But sustainability isn't just about the environment. It also encompasses social responsibility. So, think about how your advertising can reflect that. Partner with like-minded organizations for joint environmental campaigns, such as planting trees or cleaning up beaches. This not only amplifies your message but also shows that you're eager to collaborate and make a difference together.In addition to partnering with organizations, educate and empower your consumers to make sustainable choices. Provide them with information on how they can reduce waste, conserve energy, or support local communities. Empower them to be part of the solution and create a positive impact in their own lives.

Now, I know what you might be thinking - "But how do I measure the impact of sustainability-focused advertising?" Great question! Like any other marketing effort, measuring the effectiveness of sustainability-focused advertising requires tracking and evaluating key metrics. Monitor changes in consumer behaviour, such as an increase in sales of eco-friendly products or an uptick in website

traffic after running sustainability-focused campaigns. Don't forget to survey your customers to gauge their awareness and perception of your sustainability efforts.

Remember, sustainability is an ever-evolving area, and the trends and expectations will change over time. So, keep your finger on the pulse and adapt your advertising strategies accordingly. Stay informed about the latest sustainability initiatives and consumer expectations. Evolve your messaging and campaigns as needed to stay relevant and resonate with your audience.

Finally, sustainability is not a solo endeavour. It's a collective effort. Collaborate with your team, engage stakeholders, and involve your customers in the process. By working together, you can build a sustainable future for your business and the planet.

And that wraps up Chapter 18, my friends! We've explored the importance of embracing sustainability in your advertising strategies, how to incorporate sustainability messaging authentically, and the measurement of sustainability-focused advertising. Remember, sustainability isn't just a buzzword - it's a mindset that can drive long-term success and make a positive impact on the world.

In Chapter 19, we'll delve into developing a crisis communication plan to ensure that your advertising efforts can weather any storm. Stay tuned, marketing mavericks, because there's more exciting knowledge to come!

CHAPTER 19: DEVELOPING A CRISIS COMMUNICATION PLAN

Where information travels at the speed of light, a well-prepared crisis communication plan is absolutely essential for any business. No matter how well your advertising strategies may be working, you never know when something unexpected could happen that requires a swift and strategic response.

Think about it - a product recall, a data breach, a scandal involving a key executive - these are all situations that can happen to any business, big or small. And when they do, how you respond can make all the difference in preserving your brand's reputation and maintaining the trust of your customers.

So, let's dive right in and talk about the key steps in developing a crisis communication plan.

Step 1: Understanding the need for crisis communication

First things first, it's important to understand why crisis communication is so crucial. When a crisis hits, people want information and reassurance. They want to know that you're taking the situation seriously and that you're doing everything possible to address the issue. If you fail to communicate effectively during a crisis, it can lead to speculation, rumours, and even more damage to your brand's reputation.

Step 2: Identifying potential crisis scenarios and risks

The next step is to identify the potential crisis scenarios that your business could face. This could include things like product recalls, negative media coverage, legal issues, or even natural disasters. Assessing your business and industry risks will help you proactively address potential crisis situations and develop appropriate responses in advance.

Step 3: Developing a crisis communication policy and team

Now that you know what you're preparing for, it's time to develop a crisis communication policy and assemble a crisis communication team. This team should consist of key individuals from various departments within your organization, including PR, marketing, legal, and senior management. Together, they will be responsible for creating and implementing the crisis communication plan when the need arises.

Step 4: Creating effective crisis messaging and responses

When a crisis occurs, it's important to have a clear and concise messaging framework in place. Your crisis communication team should develop key messages that address the situation, demonstrate empathy, and outline the steps your organization is taking to rectify the issue. These messages should be consistent across all communication channels, including press releases, social media, and internal memos.

Step 5: Utilizing various channels in crisis communication

Speaking of communication channels, it's important to have a well-defined strategy for using different channels during a crisis. Social media can be especially powerful in getting your message out quickly, but it can also be a double-edged sword if not handled carefully. Your crisis communication plan should outline guidelines for using each channel, as well as establish protocols for monitoring and responding to social media activity.

Step 6: Monitoring and evaluating crisis communication efforts

Once the dust has settled and the crisis has been resolved, it's important to take the time to evaluate your crisis communication efforts. This will help you identify any areas of improvement and incorporate those learnings into your plan for the future. Keep in mind that a crisis communication plan is not a one-time thing; it needs to be regularly reviewed and updated to stay relevant.

Remember, a crisis communication plan is not just about firefighting in the heat of the moment. It's about being proactive, prepared, and transparent. By having a well-thought-out plan in place, you can minimize the impact of a crisis on your business and come out stronger on the other side.

And there you have it - an overview of developing a crisis communication plan. I hope this chapter has shed some light on why it's so important and how you can go about creating one. So go ahead, be prepared, and face any crisis head-on with confidence! Your customers and your brand will thank you for it.

CHAPTER 20: EVOLVING ADVERTISING STRATEGIES FOR LONG-TERM SUCCESS

Now, you might be thinking, "Why do I need to keep changing my advertising strategies? Can't I just find something that works and stick to it?" Well, my friend, the advertising landscape is constantly evolving. Consumer behaviours' change, technology advances, and new trends emerge. To stay ahead of the game, you need to be willing to adapt and evolve your advertising strategies.

First and foremost, it's crucial to keep up with industry trends and evolving consumer behaviours. What worked for you a few years ago may not be as effective today. By staying abreast of the latest trends and understanding how your target audience is changing, you can ensure that your advertising efforts remain relevant and impactful. Pay attention to what your competitors are doing and be on the lookout for new opportunities to engage with your customers.

Regular audits and assessments of your advertising strategies are also essential. Take a step back and evaluate the effectiveness of your current tactics. Are they still delivering the results you desire? Are there any areas for improvement? This self-reflection allows you to identify what's working well and what needs adjustment. Don't be afraid to experiment and try new approaches. Remember, progress requires taking risks and venturing into uncharted territory.

Moreover, as you evolve your advertising strategies, it's crucial to remain true to your brand's identity. While it's important to adapt to new trends and technologies, you should always stay aligned with your core values and brand messaging. Consumers appreciate consistency and authenticity, so ensure that any new advertising tactics you explore still align with your brand's mission and personality.

Balancing short-term advertising goals with long-term sustainability is another key aspect of evolving your advertising strategies. While it's important to achieve immediate results and drive sales, you should also consider the long-term implications of your advertising choices. Building a strong brand reputation and cultivating loyal customers takes time. So, make sure your advertising strategies are designed not just for short-term gains, but also to establish a solid foundation for sustained success.

Lastly, keep in mind that the advertising landscape is bound to continue evolving. New technologies, platforms, and strategies will emerge. To stay ahead, make a commitment to lifelong learning. Constantly educate yourself about industry trends, attend conferences, participate in workshops, and engage with thought leaders in the field. This ongoing education will equip you with the knowledge and insights needed to adapt your advertising strategies and remain at the forefront of your industry.

So, as we wrap up this book, remember that advertising is not a one-time effort. It's a continuous process of learning, adapting, and evolving. By keeping up with industry trends, regularly assessing your strategies, staying true to your brand's identity, balancing short-term and long-term goals, and committing to lifelong learning, you'll be well on your way to achieving long-term success in your advertising endeavours.

Congratulations on reaching the end of The Marketing Maverick!

Armed with the knowledge and insights shared in this book, you now have the tools to take your start-up's advertising to new heights. So go out there, be bold, and make your mark in the advertising world!

ABOUT THE AUTHOR

Korki Levine

In KORKI's books, you won't find complex theories or jargon-filled lectures. Instead, he takes a refreshingly down-to-earth approach, speaking directly to the reader as if they were sitting across from him at a cozy coffee shop. With warmth and humor, he tackles many of life's common challenges, providing practical advice and actionable steps to empower readers to make positive changes.

Through his conversational style, KORKI creates an immediate connection with his audience. It feels as if he's speaking directly to you, acknowledging your struggles and gently guiding you towards solutions.
His words are like a comforting hug, reminding you that you're not alone in your journey, and that growth and self-improvement are attainable goals.

KORKI'S books are a breath of fresh air amidst the overwhelming sea of literature. His conversational style disarms any skepticism or resistance, making it easy to absorb his teachings and apply them to your own life.
Whether he's discussing relationships, personal growth, or overcoming challenges, KORKI'S words resonate deeply, leaving a lasting impact on his readers.

So, if you're seeking an author who will speak to you in a genuine, relatable, and conversational way, Korki Levine is the name to look out for. His books offer a reassuring voice, guiding you towards a better version of yourself while keeping you company on your journey to personal fulfillment.